Vital

Interactive

Strategies:

Actions needed to be taken by smart people.

By

Joanna B. Clark

Disclaimer

Table of content

Introduction

Being active in dealing with high-stakes interactions, or urgent discussions, can make work and your life significantly more straightforward. It's a truly helpful quality to managers or owners of establishments and organizations. It also helps to save time and some valuable goods (money).

The qualities of being a good leader or colleague in an organization will make your work easier and keep a good interactive relationship. Do well to click on the "buy button" to access more of the strategies for a vital interaction.

What is a vital interaction?

A vital interaction is a conversation between at least two individuals where; different ideas pop up, conclusions vary and feelings differ.

The result altogether influences their lives and there is a huge gamble of unfortunate results.

There are various ways one can vitally express oneself, for instance, you might have to caution a partner with a discourteous or lackadaisical attitude or you might have to make some noise when you think there is an error in an important work or job.

Step-by-step instructions to know a vital interaction.

Some expressions will show if you should be engaged in an interaction. Those expressions will tell if the conversation is vital or not.

Physical expression - You will show the actual indication of stress and nervousness, for instance, perspiring, expanded pulse, shallow breathing, stomach hurt, dry throat, strain, and so on.

Emotional expression - You will encounter major areas of strength for a reaction for example fear or anger happiness or joy etc.

Attitudinal expressions- you might stay away from or participate in pointless ways of behaving, for example, leaving the discussion, turning out to be peaceful, not getting out whatever you truly think, raising your voice, etc.

For what reason do people default in vital interaction?

People constantly interact, however, the higher the stakes, the more value you will place on the discussion. This could be because you're accustomed to conveying in regular low-stakes trades so you have become not so much mindful but rather more programmed with your reactions.

In high-stakes discussions you should be aware of everything engaged with the correspondence, for example, considerations, feelings, words, voices, looks, and ways of behaving. As you are not used to giving such close consideration your correspondence might fizzle.

Additionally, in these circumstances, the pressure reaction is probably going to be set off and the impacts of this can prevent your correspondence; for example, your voices and looks become more enthusiastic to control, it's harder to structure contemplations, your breathing rate increases, and so forth.

The result of neglecting to convey successfully in a vital discussion can be outrageous and loads of parts of your life can be impacted, for example, your profession, connections, and well-being.

Managing vital interactions

There are three different ways of managing vital interaction:

Annulment: Performing inadequately because of: the pressure reaction being enacted, an absence of readiness - maybe the discussion began all of a sudden and you might be expected to ad-lib which you might see as troublesome.

Performing actually: You can evaluate how you normally handle an urgent discussion by pondering how you regularly oversee heated discussions: You might conceal how vexed or furious you grope and work yourself inside yet remain silent, and you might respond forcefully towards the others in question or you might talk sincerely and deferentially.

Learn more skills on the web:

Quick-track your profession with grant-winning courses and reasonable practice.

Things to be done before a vital interaction commences

Choose precisely exact thing you're managing

Is it a segregated occasion? A repeating issue? A relational issue? By determining how serious the issue is in advance you can lay out how the discussion will be taken care of. For instance, you might have to address a representative since they showed up an hour late to work one day without clarification yet this would be taken care of distinctively to somebody who has been late consistently throughout the previous fourteen days.

Comprehend the reason why you're having the conversation.

You want to enter the discussion realizing the reason why you're having it in any case and what your favored result is. Do you want additional data from the individual? Do they have to apologize? Should an arrangement be made? You want to comprehend your thinking for the discussion since this will keep you zeroed in any event when you fundamentally vary in assessment or experience compelling feelings.

Pick the perfect opportunity and area

A general setting where you can all completely take care of the discussion is required or the issue will not be managed really. Guarantee that you check with the others that they can go to at that general setting and twofold check when you meet. This assent additionally guarantees that you're undeniably dedicated to the discussion.

Lady having an essential discussion

Comprehend that everybody will find the discussion troublesome; perceive that the discussion will be similarly troublesome, perhaps more so, for the others in question so enter it with sympathy and empathy. Likewise, enter accepting that you have something to learn.

Managing qualms

You might ponder dropping the gathering yet consider the dangers of not shouting out contrasted with making some noise.

The significance of exchange

This implies that you ought to talk straightforwardly and genuinely with one another.

Discourse is intended to fill the "Pool of Shared Importance". This is where the perspectives, realities, suppositions, speculations, feelings, and encounters partook in the discussion are perceived and esteemed by all interested parties. The more prominent the common significance there is, the better the choice. Nonetheless, this isn't effortlessly accomplished because not every person feels happy with imparting their insights and perspectives.

Steps expected to oversee urgent discussions

We will cover the accompanying advances expected to oversee vital discussions:

Moving toward a critical discussion - Begin with yourself

Notice when well-being is in danger

Make it protected to share

Ace your accounts - managing compelling feelings

Talk genuinely without culpable

Investigate others' ways

Transforming vital discussions into activities

Practice troublesome discussions with VirtualSpeech.

1. Moving toward a vital discussion - Begin with yourself

At the point when you feel compromised you might leave what you need to express and on second thought decide to safeguard yourself by, for instance, keeping silent or rebuffing others. So reassuring sharing can be troublesome - the main thing you can do to guarantee discourse is to chip away at yourself.

2. Notice the indications of an urgent discussion: First become mindful of when you are engaged in a critical discussion.

Get back to exchange: Focus on your intentions as they might be creating some distance from discourse. Request that yourself the accompanying re-visitation of exchange:

What is it that I need for myself, for other people, for our relationship?
How might I act on the off chance that I truly needed this result? Deny the Sucker's Decision:

Notice when you begin talking yourself into a "Sucker's Decision" - these are either/or decisions that can be utilized to legitimize a pointless way of behaving by saying that you had no real option except to contend against or pull out - there could have been no other choice.

Check whether you're letting yourself know that you need to pick either winning or losing and genuineness and so on.

Explain what you don't need and add this to what you do need, then, at that point, find out if there's a method for achieving both and take you back to discourse:

What you need: "I maintain that Sam should be more solid. I'm exhausted from being appointed to his work at the last moment since he hasn't gotten it done."
What you don't need: "I don't need to have a heated argument which will cause strain among us and won't determine what is happening."

Requesting how to achieve both: "How might I have a legit conversation with Sam about being more solid and abstaining from causing strain and with nothing to do?"

Notice when well-being is in danger
Search for signs that individuals are frightened because this will thus demolish the nature of the discussion since they might be contemplating themselves. At the point when you feel dangerous you will fall back on one or the other quiet or savagery:

Quiet is the point at which you specifically share specific data and keep other data. You need to try not to make an issue and the others engaged in the discussion don't have the foggiest idea about your thought process subsequently decreasing the progression of importance into the pool. The three most normal types of quietness are:

Veiling: when you make light of your thoughts or you specifically show your considerations, for instance, you might be snide or gloss over.

Annulling: consists of changing the subject, not resolving the issue, or changing the concentration from yourself to other people.

Pulling out: when you leave the discussion.

Viciousness is convincing others to take on your perspectives which thus powers importance into the pool.

The three most normal types of viciousness are:

Controlling: when you pressure others to embrace your perspective, or you might hinder others, overemphasize realities and direct the conversation.

Naming: consists of putting a mark on others or thoughts so they can be excused for example ridiculing and summing up.

Going after: includes threatening or disparaging others.

To by and by defeat falling into quiet or brutality you want to self-screen by zeroing in on the thing you're doing and what impact this is having. From this, you can change your way of behaving likewise. You don't guarantee to trust that a high-risk discussion will end up beginning by doing this - begin by surveying how you respond and act when you're worried.

3. Make it protected to share

It's vital to cause everybody to feel sufficiently great to share or you risk weakening your substance or trying to say whatever is at the forefront of your thoughts with practically no worry. You want to figure out how to move back from the substance when it feels hazardous to share, make it protected and afterward return it.

Circumstances where security is in danger

There are two circumstances where security is in danger:

An absence of shared reason
An absence of shared regard

An absence of shared reason

Finding a shared object is the principal method for making a conversation safe. All of you should know that you're cooperating for a typical result and that all of you care about everybody's inclinations and values. At the point when the design is in danger there, are retentions, individuals become guarded, there are allegations, stowed away plans and you continue to show up back to a similar subject.

Check whether the common design is in danger by inquiring: Do others accept I care about their objectives in this conversation? Do they trust my goals?

An absence of common regard

At the point when there is an absence of regard then a discussion becomes about guarding pride and confidence. Recall that you don't need to concur with what somebody is expressing to regard them.

Check whether common regard is in danger by inquiring: Do others accept I regard them?

Reestablish shared reason and common regard
Reestablish shared reason and regard by:

Saying 'sorry' when you've committed an error that has adversely impacted others.

Differentiating to fix a misconception - when others feel slighted because they have misread your motivation or rationale, make sense of what you don't mean, and make sense of what you plan to do. This is a don't/do explanation where you:

Address the worries that you don't regard others or that you have a malignant reason.

Affirm your regard or explain your genuine reason.

Utilize the Bunk device to assist you with getting to a shared reason on the off chance that you are experiencing some miscommunication:

Resolve to look for a shared reason - concur that you will come to an answer that serves everybody.

perceive the reason behind the system - everybody's expectations ought to be analyzed. Ask individuals, including yourself, why they need (reason) what they're requesting (procedure). For instance, on the off chance that two individuals need the gathering room on Thursday, what they need is a confidential space. The contention isn't about the gathering room explicitly, it's tied in with having a confidential room.

Design a common reason - on the off chance that you're experiencing issues in settling on a shared reason, create one that has a more significant level/enveloping long haul objective as this is more persuading than the reasons that have kept you in struggle.

Conceptualize new methodologies - look for common arrangements.

Assemble Profession Abilities On the web

Quick-track your profession with grant-winning courses and reasonable practice.

4. **Ace your accounts** - managing compelling feelings

The higher the stakes the more troublesome it is to get a grip on your feelings and compelling feelings can prompt quiet or viciousness.

A "Way to Activity" assists you with perceiving how your contemplations, feelings, and encounters lead to your activities. A Way to Activity has the accompanying advances:

Something occurs and you see it or hear it

You recount it (you structure a translation)

You feel feelings in light of this story

You follow up on these feelings

For instance: You might see a partner going home 30 minutes ahead of schedule and you get bothered and yell at her the following day. The truth of the matter is that this individual left 30 minutes before the functioning day wrapped up. That is all you most certainly know. You then, at that point, recounted a story to yourself - that she's lethargic and childish. This drove you to be aggravated and yell.

However, you can assume back command over your feelings by recounting an alternate story and this will lead you to act all the more properly. So imagine a scenario in which you had let yourself know that the associate left since she'd got a call about her accomplice being taken to the emergency clinic and she was terrified to the point that she left the workplace without telling anybody. You would have an alternate response.

So assuming compelling feelings are driving you to quietness or brutality take a stab at going over the means that happen between your viewpoints, feelings, and conduct and pose the accompanying inquiries:

How am I acting? - Perhaps you're showing indications of quietness or brutality.

What feelings am I encountering?

What story has driven me to these feelings?

Take a gander at current realities and ask what proof I need to help this story.

Separate your understanding from the real proof - all things considered, you've recently shaped a finish of your thought process as opposed to what occurred.

Could I at any point genuinely see or hear what I'm talking about is a reality? What did I see/hear?

Reexamine your feelings by inquiring: Is this the right profound reaction to the circumstance?

Smart stories

Smart stories are everything that we say to ourselves to legitimize our way of behaving. They excuse us from assuming liability and recognizing our missteps:

Casualty stories - letting yourself know that it's not your issue, that you're honest, and that you haven't added to the issue.

Antagonist stories - faulting others for everything, deciding between them as having the absolute worst intentions, and supporting your way of behaving.

Vulnerable stories - letting yourself know that you are too feeble to do anything so you take the choice of sitting idly.

You want to transform these accounts into helpful stories so you experience less troublesome feelings subsequently prompting valuable exchange.

Transform casualties into entertainers by asking - Am I making light of my job in this issue while enhancing others' jobs? perceive that generally speaking, you have added to the issue here and there - regardless of whether this is because you didn't offer something prior.

Transform bad guys into people - how could a good individual do this? Trade your judgment with sympathy and self-legitimization with moral obligation.

Transform powerlessness into tables - What is it that I truly need for me, for other people, for our relationship? How might I act assuming I truly needed this result?

5. Talk sincerely without culpable

At the point when you have made the right condition for discourse you want to talk straightforwardly and yet not hurt others. It means a lot to "Express your way" by utilizing the STATE abilities - these are particularly valuable for dealing with delicate points. It carries the concentration to yourself so it may very well be very dismaying from the start.

Share your realities - Begin with your realities as they are the most un-disputable and enticing components of your Way to Activity. Try not to bring your translations into this.

"I've seen that you've missed the last two group gatherings."

Recount your story - make sense of what you've finished up in light of these realities yet pay special attention to any dangers and manage them if they emerge.

"As of late you've mentioned for me to send each of my drafts to you and register with you consistently about the gathering plan. I feel that you don't genuinely trust my work."

Request others' ways - request others' realities and stories.

"Do you unexpectedly see this?"

"What's happening?"

"This is how it seemed to me, have I misconstrued it?"

Talk probably - While you're sharing your story, recall that it's a translation and not a reality so don't recount the story like it's a reality. The accompanying assertions are great approaches to doing this without being excessively forceful or latent:

"I get the impression that..."

"From my place of view..."

In my opinion..."

Energize testing - Welcome contradicting perspectives and challenge your reasoning. Assuming that they appear to be hesitant to share, think about saying: "Suppose I'm mixed up. Consider the possibility that the inverse is valid."

6. Investigate others' ways

It tends to be troublesome on the off chance that individuals you're talking with are encountering a profoundly close-to-home response, or on the other hand if they're not sharing, they're exceptionally delicate, protective, etc. Arriving at an answer in these situations is hard. Four listening devices assist with empowering others to have a real sense of security to share:

Request their accounts - express revenue in hearing others' perspectives:

"I'd prefer to know what's in your mind..."

Mirror to affirm sentiments - consciously recognize the feelings they appear to be feeling.

"You look unsure..."

"You appear upset..."

Reword - Take what the other individual has said and express it in your particular way. This affirms that you're tuning in and you're attempting to completely comprehend because their perspectives are esteemed.

"So my thought process you're not kidding.."

"We should check whether I've perceived this..."

Prime - On the off chance that others keep on keeping down, state what you think the other individual is thinking. This ought to possibly be utilized on the off chance that the other three instruments haven't worked.

"I'm guessing you believe I'm being unfair..."

What if we conflict?
It's currently your chance to answer so think about utilizing the ABC strategy. This device is especially useful when a worry is imparted to you:

Concur - find where you concur.

"I concur that these most recent fourteen days have been especially difficult..."

Construct - expand on it with something they have missed or didn't have any idea.
"I'm additionally mindful that the entire branch has been chaotic in this period..."

Analyze - Look at the distinctions between your perspectives yet don't recommend others are mistaken - simply think about it.

"I can't help thinking that you feel that it's been rushed due to the progressions in structure. According to my viewpoint, this is because individuals aren't happy answering to the new boss yet."

Construct Profession Abilities On the Web
Quick-track your vocation with grant-winning courses and sensible practice.

7. Transforming significant discussions into activities

Thoughts may not be set in motion assuming individuals are uncertain of how the choice will be made and if individuals don't circle back to their guaranteed activity. Ends and choices should be explained.

Kinds of direction

There are four sorts of navigation:

Order - The power settles on the choice without the contribution of others however they make sense of their thinking.

Counsel - The power welcomes others to give data to impact them before pursuing a choice. The conference **is significant when:** many individuals are impacted by the choice, it's not difficult to accumulate the data, individuals care about the choice and there are numerous choices.

Vote - This is where a settled-upon rate swings the choice. It's pre-owned when there are areas of strength for numerous. It ought not to be utilized when individuals won't uphold the result on the off chance that it goes how they go against it - the

washouts shouldn't think often about the outcome.
Never use casting a ballot rather than exchange.

Agreement - Everybody genuinely concurs with a choice and supports it. This is just utilized for high-stakes and complex issues. It's significant not to imagine that all members will get their best option
To choose which dynamic cycle to utilize inquire:

What difference does it make? Lay out those that need to be involved, not worth including those that don't.
Who has the mastery expected to settle on the choice?
Who should concur with the choice? You could require specific specialists to collaborate.
What number of individuals ought to be involved? The inclination is to include the least number of individuals that will create an excellent choice.

Moving choice right into it - completing obviously

Who? Dispense every obligation to an individual.

What? What precisely is their obligation - Make this exceptionally understood.

By when? Set cutoff times.

Follow-up: Conclude how you will follow up and the timetable for this.

Record the choices made and each of the responsibilities guaranteed.

Consider individuals responsible for their commitments or it's the ideal opportunity for another significant discussion...

Activity focuses

To begin fostering your abilities for significant discussions, it's ideal to initially ponder how you typically answer in these circumstances and examine your viability. Consider requesting criticism from others about how they view your capacity to deal with distressing circumstances.

From this, you can find your assets and shortcomings so you'll know which regions to target. With work on overseeing essential discussions turns out to be fundamentally more straightforward and altogether less overwhelming.